Seven Wonders of

ASTEROIDS, COMETS, AND METEORS

Ron Miller

TWENTY-FIRST CENTURY BOOKS

Minneapolis

This book is dedicated to Calli and Cori Neal.

Twenty-First Century Books
A division of Lerner Publishing Group, Inc.
241 First Avenue North
Minneapolis, MN 55401 U.S.A.

Website address: www.lernerbooks.com

Library of Congress Cataloging-in-Publication Data

Miller, Ron, 1947–
    Seven wonders of asteroids, comets, and meteors / By Ron Miller.
        p.   cm. — (Seven wonders)
    Includes bibliographical references and index.
    ISBN 978-0-7613-5451-2 (lib. bdg. : alk. paper)
    1. Asteroids—Juvenile literature. 2. Comets—Juvenile literature. 3. Meteors—Juvenile literature. I. Title.
QB651.M553 2011
523.5—dc22
                                                                                                    2010015559

Manufactured in the United States of America
1 – DP – 12/31/10

Contents

INTRODUCTION

*P*EOPLE LOVE TO MAKE LISTS OF THE BIGGEST AND THE BEST. ALMOST TWENTY-FIVE HUNDRED YEARS AGO, A GREEK WRITER NAMED HERODOTUS MADE A LIST OF THE MOST AWESOME THINGS EVER BUILT BY PEOPLE. THE LIST INCLUDED BUILDINGS, STATUES, AND OTHER OBJECTS THAT WERE LARGE, WONDROUS, AND IMPRESSIVE. LATER, OTHER WRITERS ADDED NEW ITEMS TO THE LIST. WRITERS EVENTUALLY AGREED ON A FINAL LIST. IT WAS CALLED THE SEVEN WONDERS OF THE ANCIENT WORLD.

The list became so famous that people began imitating it. They made other lists of wonders. They listed the Seven Wonders of the Modern World and the Seven Wonders of the Middle Ages. People even made lists of undersea wonders and the wonders of science and technology.

But Earth doesn't contain all the wonders that have been discovered. Our planet shares the solar system with many other worlds. They all have wonderful things to see.

THE BUILDING BLOCKS OF THE SOLAR SYSTEM

After a house is built, a big pile of material is always left over. The same thing happened after the formation of the solar system. The Sun and the planets were formed from a huge cloud of dust and gas. This dust and gas came together to form tiny clumps of rock, metal, and ice. These tiny clumps gathered into bigger clumps. After millions of years, these clumps were large enough to become the Sun and the planets.

The asteroid belt in the solar system is made up of the orbiting pieces of rock, ice, and metal left over after the planets and the Sun formed. This illustration shows a view of the Sun from an asteroid.

Not all the matter in the original dust cloud was used up. Chunks of rock, metal, and ice were left over. These are what we call asteroids and comets and meteors. They are important wonders because they are remnants of the very earliest beginnings of our solar system.

1 Ceres

Ceres is the largest object in the solar system's asteroid belt. Modern astronomers have classified it as too small to be a planet.

*I*T'S A DARK NIGHT IN 1801, AND THE SICILIAN ASTRONOMER GIUSEPPE PIAZZI IS LOOKING FOR COMETS. HE NOTICES A TINY, STARLIKE OBJECT. SINCE IT MOVES SLOWLY ACROSS THE SKY FROM NIGHT TO NIGHT, HE THINKS HE HAS FOUND A NEW COMET. BUT HE DISCOVERS THAT IT HAS AN ORBIT, A PATHWAY AROUND THE SUN, MORE LIKE A PLANET THAN A COMET. HE NAMES IT CERES, AFTER THE PATRON GODDESS OF SICILY. BUT HE IS DISAPPOINTED WHEN HE CALCULATES ITS SIZE. CERES IS LESS THAN 500 MILES (800 KILOMETERS) WIDE. BARELY ONE-QUARTER THE SIZE OF EARTH'S MOON, CERES ISN'T BIG ENOUGH TO DESERVE THE NAME *PLANET*.

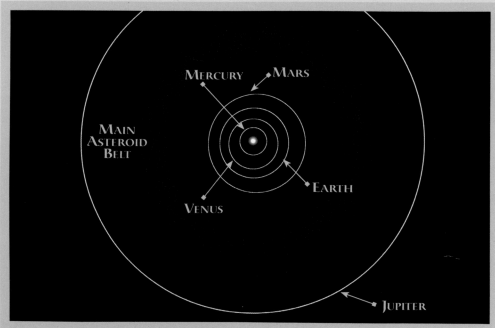

Many asteroids can be found in the asteroid belt, which orbits the Sun between Mars and Jupiter.

MORE LITTLE WORLDS

Another tiny world was found the year after Ceres was discovered. It is a little smaller than Ceres. Astronomers named it Pallas. They found two more over the next five years. Both are smaller than either Ceres or Pallas. Astraea, the fifth to be discovered, is only 100 miles (160 km) wide. These little worlds are so small that the astronomers first described them with the term *minor planets*. Most people, however, know them as asteroids, a word that means "like stars."

Modern astronomers have listed several hundred thousand asteroids. One estimate has one to two million asteroids orbiting between Mars and Jupiter. This region has become known as the asteroid belt. At least 98 percent of all known asteroids orbit there. As many as four thousand of them are larger than 0.6 mile (1 km) across. This sounds like an awful lot of material. But if every asteroid were to be combined into one big ball, it would be less than 900 miles (1,448 km) wide. This is less than half the size of Earth's Moon.

THE LARGEST ASTEROID

Ceres is the largest known asteroid. It is 568 miles (914 km) across—almost twice the size of the next-largest asteroid. It is one-fourth the size of all the asteroids in the entire asteroid belt combined. It is larger than most of the moons of Saturn and Jupiter.

FACTS ABOUT *Ceres*

Diameter: 590 miles (950 km)

Average distance from the Sun: 277 million miles (446 million km)

Length of year (the time it takes to orbit the Sun): 1,680 days

Scientists don't know much about what Ceres looks like. Even in the largest telescopes, it looks like a blurry ball with faint light and dark features. It has a large bright spot and a large dark spot. These may be giant craters on its surface. It may also have a very thin atmosphere and a rocky surface covered in frost.

This digital illustration shows the orbits of Ceres (left), *Mars* (center, closest to the Sun), *and Jupiter* (bottom right) *as they circle the Sun.*

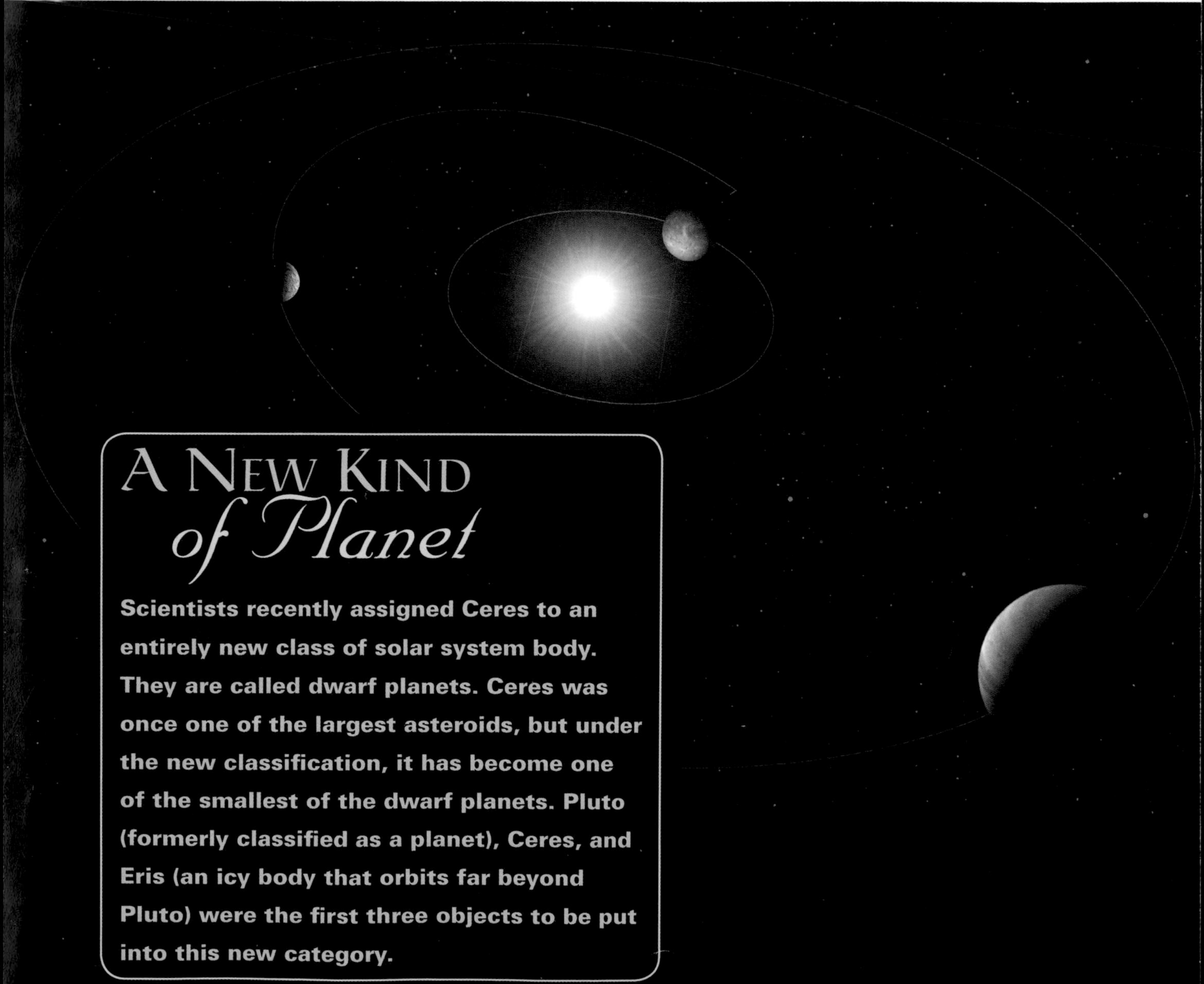

A New Kind of Planet

Scientists recently assigned Ceres to an entirely new class of solar system body. They are called dwarf planets. Ceres was once one of the largest asteroids, but under the new classification, it has become one of the smallest of the dwarf planets. Pluto (formerly classified as a planet), Ceres, and Eris (an icy body that orbits far beyond Pluto) were the first three objects to be put into this new category.

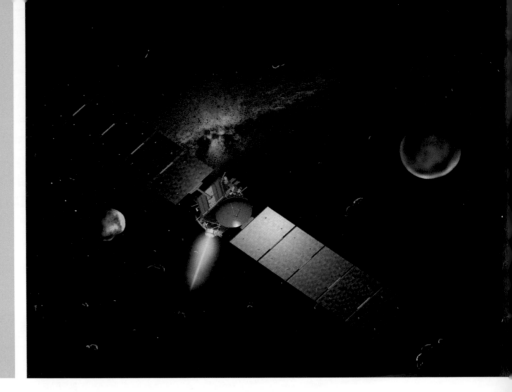

The Dawn *space probe is seen near the asteroid* Vesta (left) *and the dwarf planet* Ceres (right) *in this illustration.* Dawn *was launched in 2007.*

On September 27, 2007, the National Aeronautics and Space Administration (NASA) launched the *Dawn* spacecraft. Its mission is to explore the asteroid belt. It is scheduled to visit the asteroid Vesta in 2011 and Ceres in February 2015. As the spacecraft swings close to Ceres, it will take photos and scan the surface of the asteroid. This will help scientists learn what Ceres is made of and how it was formed.

THE ASTEROID ZOO

Asteroids come in all sizes and shapes. They range from rocks only a few hundred feet across to flying mountains 500 miles (800 km) wide. The very biggest are round. But smaller objects have weaker gravity. A large body such as Earth tends to be round. Every point on the surface of Earth is just about the same distance from the center. This is because its gravity is strong enough to flatten out any large lumps. But with much less gravity to pull at an asteroid's surface, it can be any shape at all.

The first asteroid to be explored by a spacecraft was 433 Eros. The Near Earth Asteroid Rendezvous (NEAR) *Shoemaker* spacecraft, launched in 1996,

"The asteroid belt is a great grinding mill, producing smaller and smaller pieces down to motes of dust."
—*Carl Sagan, American astronomer,* Cosmos, *1980*

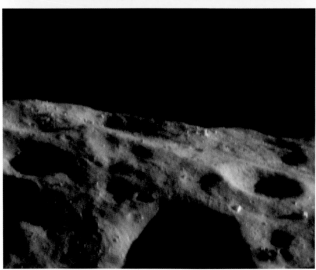

Top: *Lumpy 433 Eros was the first asteroid to be photographed up close by a spacecraft. Its saddle-shaped dent can be seen at the lower edge.*
Bottom: *The NEAR Shoemaker spacecraft took this photo of 433 Eros's horizon.*

photographed its surface. The photos showed that 433 Eros is shaped like a giant cashew nut measuring 22 × 8 × 8 miles (35 x 13 x 13 km). A deep, saddlelike dent in the middle separates two bulging ends. While the rest of Eros is heavily cratered, the saddle is remarkably smooth. The saddle might be a huge dent caused by a collision with another asteroid.

Gravity

The amount of gravity a body has depends on how much mass it has. The bigger and heavier something is, the more gravity it produces. Earth has about 6 trillion tons (5 trillion metric tons) of mass. (Mass is the amount of stuff that an object contains.) Earth's gravity makes you weigh what you do and pulls you back down when you jump. A small asteroid like 624 Hektor has much less mass than Earth. As a result, Hektor's gravity is 150 times less than Earth's. You would be able to jump from one end of Hektor to the other easily. In fact, you would have to be very careful not to launch yourself off into space!

Other asteroids have even more unusual shapes. For instance, 4179 Toutatis and 1620 Geographos are shaped like rounded-off boxcars. On the other hand, 216 Kleopatra looks like a dog bone, and 4769 Castalia resembles a hamburger bun.

An even more interesting asteroid is 624 Hektor. It is shaped like two beach balls just touching each other. It is probably the result of two asteroids colliding. But the collision was a gentle one. Instead of hitting so hard they shattered, the two asteroids stuck together. Visiting Hektor would be a weird experience. If you were to hike to the contact region, you would see a mountain of rock 93 miles (150 km) high hanging directly over your head!

Astronomers have discovered asteroids with many unusual shapes. The asteroid 216 Kleopatra resembles a dog bone.

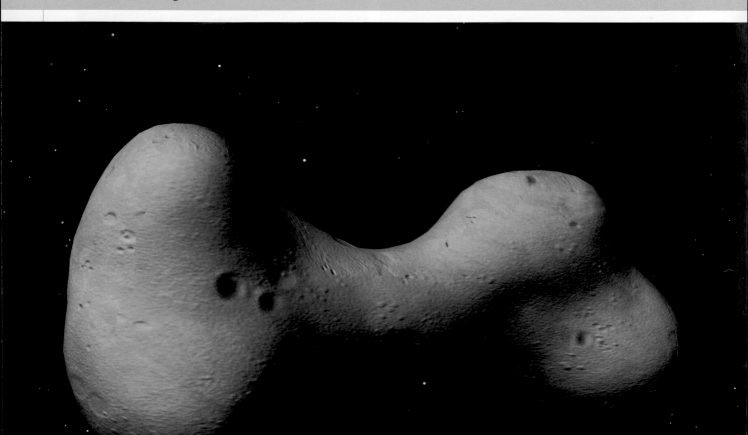

The small asteroid 243 Ida is fairly typical. It is only 20 miles (32 km) wide and shaped like a potato. It wouldn't be very interesting except for one thing:. Ida has a moon! It was discovered in 1993 by scientist Ann Harch. She had been looking closely at some photos of Ida taken by the *Galileo* spacecraft, and there it was—a tiny speck of light near the asteroid. She realized that this speck was a little moon, which she named Dactyl. It is only 0.9 miles (1.4 km) across. Since then, other asteroids have been found to have moons. Astronomers call them minor moons because they orbit minor planets.

One of the most unique of all asteroids is 25143 Itokawa. When the Japanese spacecraft *Hayabusa* visited the asteroid in 2005, it found something very strange. Most asteroids resemble relatively smooth boulders pitted with meteoroid craters of all sizes. But Itokawa has almost no craters at all. Instead, it appears to be made of thousands of loosely attached rocks and boulders. This small asteroid, measuring 1,755 × 964 × 686 feet (535 × 294 × 209 meters), may have formed when the gentle pull of its gravity caused gravel and rocks to slowly drift together.

WHERE DID THEY COME FROM?

Throughout history scientists have had many theories about the origin of the solar system and Earth. Most modern scientists tell us that the Sun and the planets formed about 4.5 billion years ago.

"The minor planets still revolving today may well be regarded as the survivors of ten thousand times as many, which once filled the sky like migrating birds."
—*Fritz Kahn, German science writer and illustrator,* Design of the Universe, *1954*

Originally there was only an enormous cloud of dust and gas. This cloud was large enough that the pull of the gravity on its particles started shrinking the cloud. As it shrank, the particles grew closer together. This increased the gravitational pull, which made the particles pull together even faster. The dust and the gas were densest in the center of the cloud. As this material became compressed, it heated up. Eventually it was hot enough to create a new star, the Sun.

Within the cloud surrounding the new sun, tiny particles of dust collided and stuck together, forming clumps of material. As these clumps—called planetesimals—grew in size, they attracted more particles. Most of these early collisions were relatively gentle, so the planetesimals didn't knock themselves into pieces. Soon grains of dust grew to the size of rocks. Then the rocks grew into boulders and then into asteroids miles across. The whole process of growing from the size of a large pinhead to a mountain may have taken one hundred thousand years or so. Then the process began to slow down. The original dust and gas had been used up, and the cloud thinned. Several stars—such as Beta Pictoris—have been observed with large, thin disks of dust surrounding them. These may be solar systems at this stage of development.

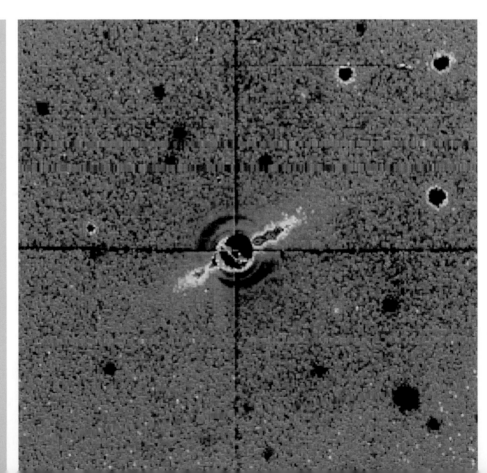

This composite image of the star Beta Pictoris shows a large disk of dust around the star. It may be that this star is another solar system more than fifty light years from Earth. A light year is the distance light travels in a year—5.9 trillion miles (9.5 trillion km).

HEATING BY *Compression*

You can see for yourself how compressing a substance can make it grow warmer. Hold a rubber ball in your hand. Rapidly squeeze it tight several times. You will feel it grow warmer. If you have a tire pump for your bicycle, you can do a similar experiment. Pump air very quickly and then feel the side of the pump. It will have grown very warm. This is because the air inside the pump warmed as it was compressed, just like the dust and the gas in the early solar system.

Some of the planetesimals eventually grew into huge bodies that became planets like Earth. But once the planets finished forming, there was still a lot of material left over. Some of this was rock and metal, and some was ice. As the new planets orbited the Sun, they swept up most of these leftovers. The biggest planet, Jupiter, was very good at this. We live in a much cleaner solar system than the one that existed one billion years ago. This is a very good thing. No one wants mountain-sized rocks falling from the sky every day. Most of the planetesimals that weren't absorbed by Earth, Mars, Jupiter, and the other planets settled in the asteroid belt.

Most asteroids remained very small, but some grew to be giants. Ceres, Vesta, and Pallas are the three largest asteroids. We on Earth are lucky that these and most other big asteroids orbit within the asteroid belt, millions of miles from Earth.

2 Ganymed AND OTHER EARTHGRAZERS

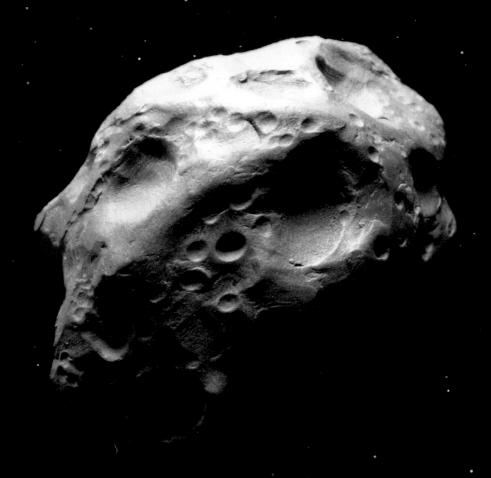

In this painting, the asteroid 1036 Ganymed (top)
is passing near the the planet Mars (bottom right).
Ganymed is a huge rock nearly 20 miles (33 km) wide.

$\mathcal{M}$OST ASTEROIDS CAN BE FOUND IN THE MAIN ASTEROID BELT. IT LIES BETWEEN TWO AND FOUR TIMES FURTHER AWAY FROM THE SUN THAN EARTH DOES. BUT NOT ALL ASTEROIDS ORBIT THERE. A SPECIAL GROUP OF ASTEROIDS ARE CALLED EARTHGRAZERS. THIS DOESN'T MEAN THAT THEY ACTUALLY GRAZE EARTH. IT MEANS THAT THEY COME VERY CLOSE TO OUR PLANET. SCIENTISTS USUALLY CALL THEM BY THE MORE ACCURATE NAME: NEAR-EARTH OBJECTS, OR NEOs.

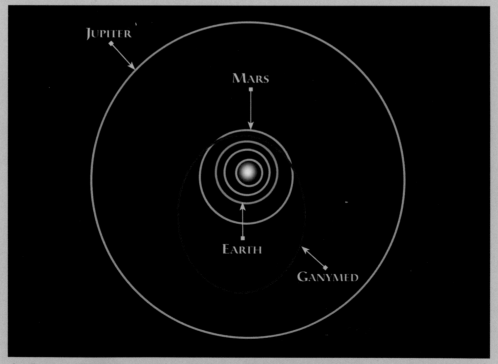

As Ganymed travels around the Sun, its orbit passes through the orbit of Mars and close to Earth's orbit.

When asteroids were first discovered, they were thought to be neatly gathered within the asteroid belt. This changed in 1898, when astronomers discovered Eros. Eros's orbit crosses the orbit of Mars. Then, in 1932, astronomers found an asteroid that crosses Earth's orbit. The asteroid was named 1862 Apollo. All asteroids that cross Earth's orbit are called Apollo asteroids. The orbits of other Apollo asteroids lie entirely within Earth's orbit.

So far, scientists have found more than 260 Apollo asteroids. They estimate there may be as many as one thousand altogether. The biggest of the Apollo asteroids to come near the orbit of Earth is 1036 Ganymed. It is a mass of solid rock nearly 19 miles

MORE THAN ONE *Ganymede*

Ganymede is a popular name in astronomy. In Greek mythology, Ganymede was taken by Zeus (or Jupiter, in Roman tales) to be cupbearer to the gods. This relationship with Jupiter was probably the reason one of Jupiter's moons was named Ganymede. Walter Baade named the asteroid he discovered in 1924 after Ganymede too, though that asteroid is usually spelled Ganymed.

1862 Apollo was the first asteroid discovered to have an orbit that crosses Earth's orbit. Eros was the first asteroid found to cross the orbit of Mars. Since then astronomers have found hundreds more, some of which are shown in this diagram.

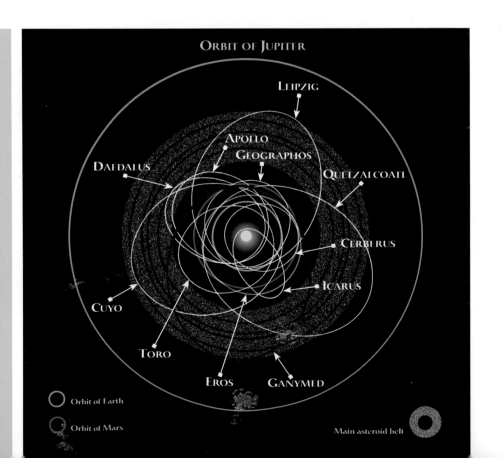

> *"Can Earth pass through so populated a space and undergo no collisions? Of course not."*
>
> —American scientist and author *Isaac Asimov*, A Choice of Catastrophes, *1979*

(30 km) in diameter. The next largest is 1862 Apollo itself, at 6 × 19 miles (10 × 30 km).

There are two ways an asteroid's orbit can cross that of Earth. It can fly above or below it, like a car crossing a railroad track by passing over it on a bridge or under it through a tunnel. Although the paths cross, there is never any danger of collision because the train and the car are on different levels. But an asteroid could also pass right across the same track Earth is on, causing a collision.

The largest known asteroid that orbits level with Earth is 1627 Ivar. It is about 5 miles (8 km) in diameter. If something this size were ever to hit Earth, it would be a global disaster. Fortunately, most near-Earth objects are less than 1.3 miles (2 km) wide. Scientists estimate that only about five asteroids large enough to do global damage hit Earth every million years. So the chances of this happening in your lifetime are pretty slim.

CLOSE CALLS

Earth seems to lie within a swarm of asteroids. Happily for us, this swarm is one thousand times less dense than the asteroid belt. Still, a lot of small bodies zoom past Earth every year—sometimes too close for comfort.

THE SMALLEST *Asteroid*

One of the smallest asteroids is an Earthgrazer discovered in 1991, when it passed Earth at a distance of just 106,191 miles (170,900 km). This is less than half the distance to the Moon. Named 1991 BA, it is only about 20 feet (6 meters) across. The orbit of 1991 BA takes it from far beyond the asteroid belt to close to the orbit of Venus. If 1991 BA were to hit Earth, it would explode with the force of 40,000 tons (40,641 metric tons) of TNT. This is about three times the energy of the first atomic bomb dropped on Hiroshima, Japan, in 1945, near the end of World War II (1939–1945). Since 1991 BA also crosses the orbits of Venus and Mars. Perhaps it will hit one of those planets instead.

Ganymed and Other Earthgrazers

19

> "What happens if a big asteroid hits Earth? Judging from realistic simulations involving a sledgehammer and a common laboratory frog, we can assume it will be pretty bad."
>
> —Dave Barry, U.S. humorist (n.d.)

In 1994 a very small asteroid passed within one-third the distance between Earth and the Moon, about 80,000 miles (128,700 km) away. A few small asteroids have even skimmed over Earth's atmosphere, like a stone skipping across the water of a pond.

On October 8, 2009, a small asteroid about 30 feet (10 m) in diameter exploded over Indonesia. The explosion was equivalent to 50,000 tons (50,802 metric tons) of TNT. Fortunately, the explosion occurred high enough above Earth that no damage resulted on the ground. Just over a month later, another small asteroid exploded over Utah. The explosion occurred at midnight, and for a brief moment the landscape was lit as bright as day.

None of these close calls would have caused worldwide damage if they had been direct hits. But they would have been able to wipe out a city or town. At present, scientists have no way to detect objects like these early enough to warn people. NASA and other government agencies are working hard to develop an asteroid warning system.

ASTEROIDS LIKE Grains of Sand

A space telescope called the Wide-field Infrared Survey Explorer (WISE) discovered more than 25,000 new asteroids in its first six months of operation. In addition to all the new asteroids, WISE also discovered fifteen new comets. The telescope was launched in December 2009. It orbits 300 miles (483 km) above Earth. Among the thousands of asteroids it has discovered, about ninety-five fall in the near-Earth object, or Earth-grazer, category. This means they can approach within 30 million miles (48 million km) of our planet. But there's no need to fear a collision. That's still 120 times farther away than the Moon. Close enough, however, for NASA to want to keep a careful watch on them.

Spaceguard

Observatories, amateur astronomers, and other groups around the world are keeping an eye out for Earthgrazing asteroids. They form an unofficial organization called Spaceguard. There are Spaceguard observatories in the United Kingdom, Germany, Japan, and several other nations. The Spaceguard Foundation, based in Italy, keeps track of all the reports. The Spaceguard network hopes to be able to discover any potentially dangerous asteroids in time to warn governments on Earth.

This painting imagines what an asteroid collision with Earth would look like. In 2009 a small asteroid just missed Earth's surface, exploding high in the atmosphere over Indonesia.

3 HALLEY'S Comet

Halley's comet streaks through
Earth's sky every seventy-five years.
The most recent visit was in 1986.

SOMETIMES AN INTRIGUING VISITOR APPEARS IN THE NIGHT SKY. IT LOOKS LIKE A STAR WITH A LONG, GLOWING TRAIL BEHIND IT. THE ANCIENT GREEKS CALLED THESE VISITORS COMETS. THIS COMES FROM A WORD MEANING "HAIRY" OR "BEARDED," BECAUSE COMET TAILS LOOK LIKE LONG, FLOWING HAIR.

In 1704 British astronomer Edmond Halley discovered that comets travel in long, egg-shaped orbits around the Sun. When he worked out the paths of four famous comets—those seen in 1456, 1531, 1607, and 1682—he found they all had the same orbit. They appeared about seventy-five years apart. Halley realized that these were not four separate comets. They were one comet that appeared over and over again as it swung around the Sun. He predicted that the comet would appear again in 1758. And on Christmas night of that year, the comet returned. It was named Halley's comet in his honor.

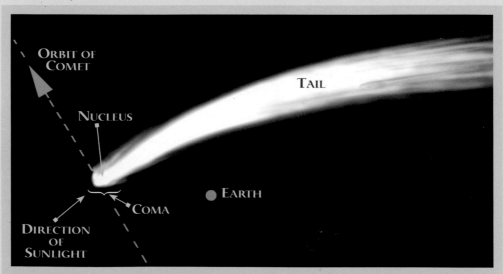

As a small, dark comet nears the Sun, the heat and solar wind create a long, visible vapor trail, the comet's tail.

> *"I came in with Halley's comet in 1835. It's coming again next year, and I expect to go out with it. The Almighty has said no doubt, 'Now here are these two unaccountable freaks; they came in together, they must go out together.'"*
>
> —*American writer Mark Twain, 1909*

American author Mark Twain was very proud of having been born in 1835, when Halley's comet blazed through the night. By a strange coincidence, Twain died in 1910, the next time the comet made an appearance in the night sky of Earth.

Astronomer Fred Whipple said comets are little more than "dirty snowballs." They are more like enormous icebergs composed of a mixture of ice; frozen gases; dark, carbon-rich compounds; rocks; and gravel. Most comets are only 0.6 to 12 miles (1 to 19 km) wide. This is much too small to be seen with telescopes. A comet only becomes visible when it heads toward the Sun and warms up.

THE COMET NURSERY

Some material left over from the formation of the solar system wound up far beyond Pluto. This is where most of the icy bodies can be found. They surround the solar system like a vast swarm of bees. Every once in a while one of these icy mountains will fall toward the Sun. When it does, we call it a comet.

Beyond Pluto, sunlight is much too weak to provide any warmth. The ice in comets

COMA (GAS HALO)

OUTER CRUST

JETS

ICE AND ROCK

NUCLEUS

One astronomer compared a comet to a dirty snowball. The central nucleus of a comet is mostly ice and rock, as illustrated above.

orbiting there is frozen as hard as steel. But when a comet comes to within about three times Earth's distance from the Sun, it starts to warm up. Some of its ice begins to turn to gas. (In the vacuum of space, water skips melting into a liquid and goes directly to gas.)

The closer the comet gets to the Sun, the more ice turns to gas. This gas forms a kind of halo around the comet called a coma. The coma glows brightly in sunlight. This is what astronomers see—not the tiny, dark nucleus of ice and rock in the center.

As the comet gets ever closer to the Sun, the coma gets larger and larger. It eventually becomes hundreds and even thousands of miles wide. The gases start to form a long, flowing tail. This tail is caused by the solar wind (a stream of particles emitted by the Sun). The tail of a comet is like a flag blowing in the wind. It may be millions or even tens of millions of miles long.

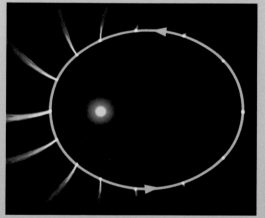

Left: *As a comet nears the Sun, its coma blows back into a long glowing tail.*
Bottom: *Comet McNaught P1 and its glowing tail passed over Australia in 2007.*

The Bayeux Tapestry, an embroidered history of the 1066 French invasion of England, includes a depiction of Halley's comet, which passed Earth that year. The Latin writing in this scene means "these men wonder at the star."

MR. HALLEY'S WONDERFUL COMET

Once astronomers knew the orbit of Halley's comet, they looked for even earlier records of it in history. The oldest they found was in 240 B.C. in China.

In 1066 it appeared in the sky during William the Conqueror's invasion of England. The famous Bayeux Tapestry, which illustrates the story of that invasion, shows people amazed by the wonderful sight in the sky.

Halley's most recent visit was in 1986. Millions of people all over the world watched it, and spacecraft were sent to meet it. When the *Giotto* spacecraft flew past Halley's comet, it revealed a very strange-looking object. The nucleus was a black, peanut-shaped body about 9 miles (14 km) long and 5 miles (8 km) wide. The surface was black because of the crust of dark, sooty dirt left behind by the evaporating ice. Huge jets of gas erupted from the surface and shot off for miles in all directions. The streams of gas finally curved back because of the pressure of the solar wind. These streams combined to form Halley's long tail. The next time the comet will be visible in Earth's sky will be in 2061.

BAD LUCK *Comets*

For thousands of years, comets were considered to be omens of disaster. It was believed they brought diseases, pestilence, and war, as poet John Milton wrote in 1667 in *Paradise Lost*. In 1910, as Earth passed through the tail of Halley's comet, some people feared that everyone on Earth might be poisoned. But the tail of a comet is much too thin to do any harm even if it did contain poisonous gases. Even as recently as 1998, some people were predicting global catastrophes on the appearance of another comet, Comet Hale-Bopp. Nothing happened, of course.

THE BIGGEST *Comet*

A comet seen in 1729—sometimes known as Comet Sarabat after an astronomer who studied it—was the largest ever observed. Modern astronomers believe that the comet's nucleus may have been 60 miles (97 km) wide.

Left: *The space probe* Giotto *flew close to Halley's comet in 1985 and took photos of its nucleus* (above).
Below: *Halley's comet was photographed in 1985 from Caltech's Palomar Observatory in San Diego County, California.*

Present-day astronomers know of at least two thousand comets. All of them are in orbit around the Sun. Some of them return every few years. Many make just one appearance and are never seen again.

THE INCREDIBLE DISAPPEARING COMET

Every time a comet passes through the inner solar system, it shrinks a little. As much as 3 feet (1 m) of its surface might be lost as its ice is evaporated by the Sun. A comet will eventually lose so much ice that it will simply fall apart. All that might be left of it is a cloud of loose gravel and rocks. Imagine a melting snowball with a lot of stones in it. A comet the size of Halley's might last for only a few thousand orbits.

Comets are also very fragile. If one passes too close to a large planet like Jupiter, the powerful gravity of the planet will cause the comet to shatter. In 1992 Comet Shoemaker-Levy 9 passed too close to Jupiter and was torn into twenty smaller

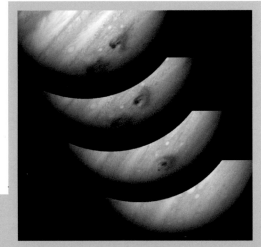

Top right: *Jupiter, with impact wounds from the break-up of comet Shoemaker-Levy 9 in 1992.*
Bottom right: *This close-up photo shows one of the impact wounds on Jupiter.*
Below: *Fragments of Shoemaker-Levy dot the night sky.*

Top: *Comet Schwassman-Wachmann 3 was photographed as it began to break up in 1995. The streaks in the background are stars.*
Left: *By 2010 Schwassmann-Wachmann 3 had broken into more than sixty pieces as it continued its orbit around the Sun.*

pieces. Two years later, these pieces ran into Jupiter, one after the other. The result was a series of gigantic explosions. These were so powerful that they were clearly seen through telescopes on Earth, nearly 400 million miles (644 million km) away. The explosions left huge, dark marks in the cloud deck that covers Jupiter. Each of these was about the size of the Pacific Ocean.

In 1995 Comet Schwassmann-Wachmann 3 began to break up. By 2006 it had shattered into more than a dozen pieces. In 2010 more than sixty pieces remain in its orbit around the Sun. Eventually nothing will be left at all.

THE SUNGRAZERS

Some comets swing so close to the Sun that they are torn apart and destroyed by the Sun's gravity. The most famous of these comet pieces are called the Kreutz Sungrazers. They are parts of a much larger comet that broke up into many smaller ones in the year 1106. A large, bright comet seen by the Greek scientist-philosopher Aristotle in 371 B.C. might have been the original. Some of the pieces became famous comets in their own right. These include the extremely bright comets seen in 1843 and 1882 and Comet Ikeya-Seki, seen in 1965. Comet Ikeya-Seki traveled as close as 280,000 miles (450,600 km) from the surface of the Sun. The gravity and heat broke it into three pieces. These pieces continued in the same orbit as the original comet and were soon lost to sight as they passed into the outer solar system. They will not come near the Sun again for nearly a thousand years.

Other comets have actually collided with the Sun itself. They disappear like snowballs tossed into a furnace!

A comet that collides with the Sun immediately melts in the Sun's enormous heat, as shown in this illustration.

DEEP *Impact*

When NASA's *Deep Impact* spacecraft visited Comet Tempel 1 in 2005, it launched a special probe called an impactor toward the comet. It hit the nucleus at several thousand miles (km) an hour *(below)*. The probe left a crater more than 650 feet (198 m) in diameter and 100 to 160 feet (30 to 49 m) deep. The cloud of debris that it created was analyzed by instruments on the spacecraft. For the first time, scientists were able to study the chemical composition of a comet's nucleus.

EXPLORING COMETS

Halley's comet was the first comet to be visited by spacecraft. When it last visited our area of the solar system, no fewer than five spacecraft flew past it. The European Space Agency's *Giotto* spacecraft was the first ever to send back close-up photos of a comet's nucleus.

In 2004 NASA's *Stardust* explorer reached Comet Wild 2. *Stardust* took pictures of Wild's nucleus. It also collected samples of the dust and gas ejected by the comet. It returned these samples to Earth, where scientists continue to study them.

NASA's space probe Stardust *flew close enough to Comet Wild 2 in 2004 to collect dust particles and gases flowing from the comet.*

"We saw kilometer-sized [0.6-mile] deep holes bounded by vertical and even overhanging cliffs; flat topped hills surrounded by cliffs; spiky pinnacles hundreds of meters tall, pointed skyward; in addition to the numerous jets of dust and gas escaping into space."
—Dr. Don Brownlee, NASA's Stardust principal investigator, October 29, 2009

ASTEROID OR COMET?

When astronomers discovered Chiron in 1979, they thought it was an asteroid. Then they realized that its orbit was unlike that of any other asteroid. Most asteroids lie within the orbit of Jupiter. But Chiron's orbit was much farther out, between Saturn and Uranus. Then the astronomers noticed something. As Chiron's orbit took it closer to the Sun, it grew brighter. It became three times brighter than it should have if it were an ordinary asteroid.

Chiron, astronomers decided, must contain ice. As it gets closer to the Sun, the ice warms up and evaporates. The resulting cloud of ice and dust surrounding Chiron makes it glow brightly. But this is exactly what comets do. This meant that as Chiron got closer to the Sun, the asteroid turned into a

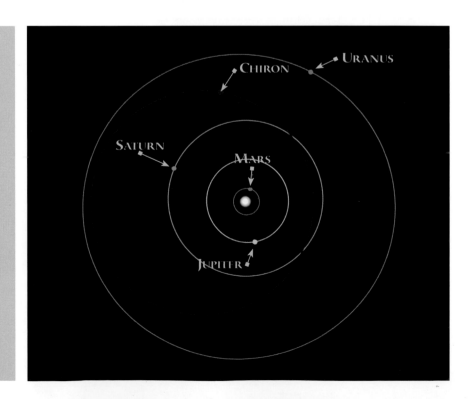

Chiron's orbit passes through Saturn's orbit and then far out beyond Saturn toward Uranus.

Sometime in the future, Chiron may come so close to Saturn that the planet's gravity will send the comet out into space or toward the Sun.

comet. This is something scientists had never before seen. Chiron is about 155 miles (249 km) wide. If it is a comet, it's the largest one known.

Scientists were lucky to have found Chiron. Its orbit is unstable. Every few thousand years, it comes close to Saturn. Sometime within the next million years, it will get so close that Saturn's gravity will throw Chiron out of the solar system. Or it might throw it toward the Sun. If this happens, it will be the brightest comet ever seen as it passes by Earth.

Since the discovery of Chiron, many similar objects have been discovered within the asteroid belt itself. The asteroid belt was long thought to consist of nothing but rocky and metallic bodies. The existence there of asteroids like Chiron shows that there may be a lot more water in the asteroid belt—in the form of ice—than anyone had ever thought. Chiron has also shown scientists that there may not be a sharp division between the objects called asteroids and comet. There may be cometlike asteroids and asteroidlike comets.

Halley's Comet

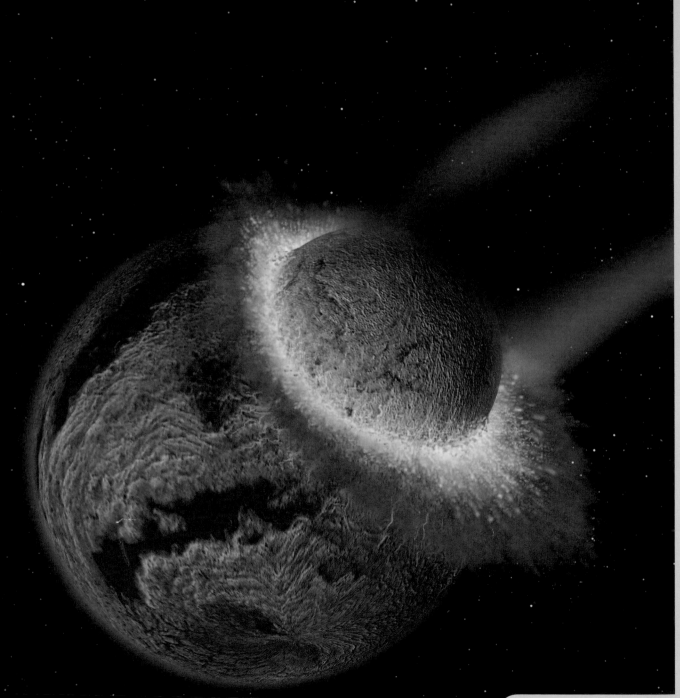

A large asteroid collided with Mars billions of years ago, creating the Borealis Basin.

*T*HE SOLAR SYSTEM IS LIKE A CROWDED HIGHWAY. ALMOST ALL THE PLANETS AND MOONS AND ASTEROIDS QUIETLY GO ABOUT THEIR ORBITS. THERE IS NO DANGER OF ONE RUNNING INTO ANOTHER. BUT JUST AS THERE ARE BAD DRIVERS ON THE HIGHWAY, THE SOLAR SYSTEM IS FILLED WITH OBJECTS THAT ZOOM ACROSS THE LANES RECKLESSLY. AND SO, JUST LIKE ON THAT BUSY HIGHWAY, ACCIDENTS HAPPEN.

Sometimes these accidents are collisions in the solar system. A disaster usually results. (The word *disaster* comes from Latin words meaning "evil star.") The collision of a planet with an asteroid causes an explosion that creates a huge hole in the planet. Some of these holes—called craters—are gigantic. The largest crater anyone knows about is on Mars. It is called the Borealis Basin.

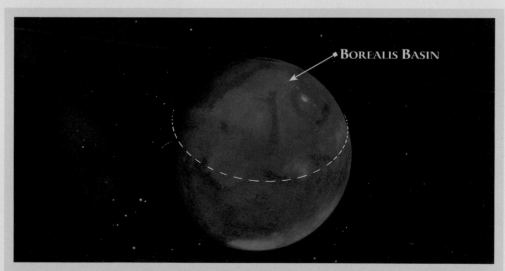

The dotted line shows the outline of the Borealis Basin on Mars. The crater has filled in during the billions of years since the impact of an asteroid with the planet. In the twenty-first century, only the rim of the basin is faintly visible.

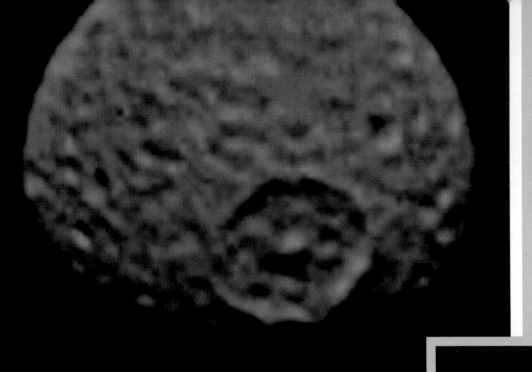

The crater is 5,300 miles (8,500 km) across and covers nearly 40 percent of the surface of Mars. It is the size of Asia, Europe, and Australia combined. The asteroid that created it was probably at least 1,200 miles (1,930 km) across.

Some craters are smaller than the Borealis Basin of Mars, but they are much bigger compared with the size of the body they're on. Mimas, a moon of Saturn, is a ball of ice only 310 miles (498 km) wide. Its most distinctive feature is a crater nearly a quarter the diameter of the little moon. It was created when an asteroid slammed into Mimas. The crater is 81 miles (130 km) wide and 5.6 miles (9 km) deep. In the center is a tall peak over 13,000 feet (3,960 m) high.

The crater Stickney on Phobos, one of the moons of Mars, is so large that it nearly split the moon in two when it was created. It is 5.6 miles (9 km) in diameter. Phobos is only 17 miles (27 km) across at its widest point.

"The impact that created Borealis Basin blasted half the surface off Mars."
—*William K. Hartmann, U.S. astronomer, 2010*

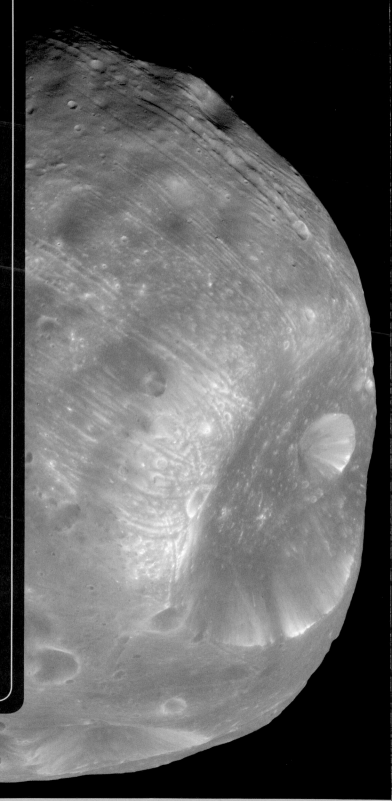

Meteor, Meteoroid, Meteorite, or Asteroid?

Most people use the word *meteor* when talking about anything involving rocks falling from the sky. But scientists make a distinction. A meteoroid is a small chunk of rock or metal flying around in space. A meteor is the streak of light seen in the sky when a meteoroid hits Earth's atmosphere and burns up. A particularly bright, impressive meteor is called a fireball. A meteorite is a piece of the meteoroid found after it has fallen to the ground.

Asteroids are much larger than meteoroids. Most meteoroids are the size of a grain of sand. Anything over a few feet in size is usually referred to as an asteroid. There is no official size limit, however. So some astronomers might call a rock 10 feet (3 m) wide a meteoroid, while others might call it an asteroid.

The Stickney crater (on the right of this image) *is the largest feature on tiny Phobos, one of the moons of Mars.*

THE LARGEST CRATER ON THE MOON

Earth's Moon has some enormous craters on it too. You can see many of them with an ordinary pair of binoculars. Near the center of the Moon (as seen from Earth) is a large crater named Copernicus. It is 58 miles (93 km) wide, about the same size as Yellowstone National Park. Another impressive crater is Tycho. It is a dazzlingly bright spot near the southern edge of the Moon. It was created about 200 million years ago when a small asteroid struck. It left a hole 52 miles (84 km) wide and 3 miles (4.8 km) deep.

This photo of the Moon shows two of its largest impact craters. Copernicus is the bright spot left of center and Tycho is the bright spot at lower center.

THE HOLE IN
the Moon

The second-largest crater in the entire solar system is on the side of the Moon we don't see from Earth. It is called the South Pole-Aitken Basin. It was created 3.9 billion years ago while the Moon was still young *(below)*. It is an enormous hole 1,550 miles (2,494 km) wide and 8 miles (13 km) deep. It is the deepest basin in the entire solar system. Since the Moon itself is only 2,159 miles (3,475 km) wide, you can get some idea of how big this impact must have been. The asteroid that created the basin punched a deep hole into the Moon. It was so deep, molten lava from the Moon's interior poured out onto the surface. It filled most of the basin. This created at broad, flat plane of smooth rock called a sea.

The largest crater on the Moon visible from Earth is Bailly. It is much harder to see than Copernicus and Tycho, however, because it lies near the visible edge of the Moon. This distorts it and makes it looks very flat. If you could see it from overhead, you would see a crater 188 miles (303 km) wide. It is about the same size as the state of Ohio. Created 3 billion years ago, it is much older than either Copernicus or Tycho.

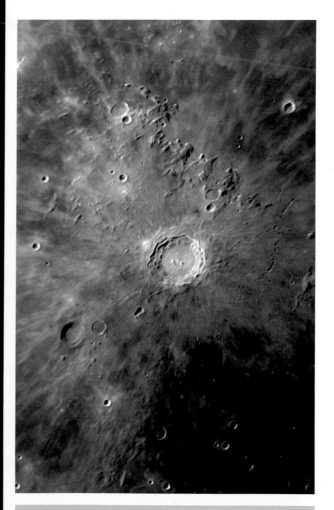

This close-up of the Moon's Copernicus crater (above) shows the crater surrounded by debris from the original asteroid impact.

The Largest Crater on Earth

Earth also has been hit by meteoroids and asteroids. An atmosphere of dense gas protects it from all but the very largest impacts. Every now and then, a meteoroid is big enough to punch through Earth's atmosphere and reach the ground. It can be traveling as fast as 75,000 miles (120,700 km) an hour when it hits Earth. When a rock weighing more than 350 tons (318 metric tons) hits at such a speed, it will explode. This happened twenty thousand years ago in Arizona. A meteoroid 150 feet (50 m) wide blasted a hole in the desert 0.5 miles (0.8 km) wide and 570 feet (170 m) deep. Known as Meteor Crater, it is one of the most popular tourist attractions in Arizona.

Scientists have discovered more than 150 craters on Earth. They range in size from just a few hundred feet to 85 miles (137 km) across or more. Over millions of years, erosion from weather, plant life, and geological forces such as volcanoes has erased signs of most of the other craters that once existed on Earth.

But that's not to say the danger no longer exists. Every year

Searching for Craters

Because erosion has erased most outward signs, ancient meteoroid craters on Earth are very hard to find. Scientists have been using satellite imagery to locate them from space. These photos reveal details that are difficult to see from ground level. As recently as 2008, for instance, a geologist located a crater in Australia. It is just 886 feet (270 m) wide and was probably created between ten thousand and one hundred thousand years ago. In 2006 a crater was found in the Sahara in Africa. That crater is 19 miles (31 km) across. Meteor Crater, in Arizona, is only 0.5 miles (0.8 km) wide.

Manicouagan Crater in northern Canada is one of the largest impact craters known on Earth. It was created when an asteroid 3 miles (5 km) wide hit Earth around 210 million years ago. The original crater was 43 miles (69 km) wide. In the twenty-first century, the crater is home to a ring-shaped lake. It wasn't until scientists saw it from space that they realized the lake was in a crater.

More craters are being found all the time as scientists search through satellite photos taken of Earth's surface from space. They show that Earth was not immune to the impact of giant meteoroids and asteroids.

eighteen thousand to eighty-four thousand meteoroids weighing more than 0.3 ounces (10 grams) hit Earth. Almost all of these are so small that they burn up in the atmosphere. Meteoroids large enough to make it to the ground are very rare.

The biggest meteoroid crater on Earth that is still visible is in South Africa. The Vredefort Crater is 186 miles (299 km) wide. It was created when a 6-mile-wide (10 km) asteroid hit Earth about 2 billion years ago. About 17 cubic miles (71 cu. km) of rock was instantly vaporized in the explosion. The crater was so big that even after billions of years of erosion, signs of it are still visible.

Left: *Vredefort Crater in South Africa is the largest crater still visible on Earth.*
Below: *Meteor Crater in Arizona is the best preserved crater in the United States. The crater was formed twenty thousand years ago.*

Only the very largest impacts on Earth have left signs that are still visible. In 2006 scientists discovered a giant impact crater buried almost 1.2 miles (2 km) under the ice of Antarctica. The crater is 310 miles (499 km) wide. Although not visible from the surface, it's the largest known crater on Earth. The asteroid that made it was almost 30 miles (48 km) wide—much bigger than the 6-mile (10 km) one that killed off the dinosaurs 65 million years ago.

THE FUTURE

The greatest worry scientists have about comets and asteroids involves one hitting a city with the kind of impact that made 1,000-mile-wide (1,609 km) holes in the Moon and Mars. This threat seemed pretty unlikely until 1994. Two years earlier, Comet Shoemaker-Levy 9 had broken into twenty pieces. In July 1994, these pieces slammed into Jupiter one after another, like the cars in a train. The resulting explosions were so large they could be seen from Earth. Together, the marks left in Jupiter's atmosphere were as big as the entire planet Earth. A comet like that hitting Earth would cause worldwide devastation.

The Shoemaker-Levy impact was not unique. Another comet or possibly an asteroid the size of several football fields hit Jupiter in July 2009. It left another planet-sized mark in the heavy cloud blanket that covers Jupiter.

AVOIDING CATASTROPHE

The collision of Comet Shoemaker-Levy 9 with Jupiter clearly showed that giant impacts are still a danger. If the comet had hit Earth instead of Jupiter, it would have been a worldwide calamity. Scientists have been anxious to discover ways to prevent this from happening. But first, astronomers need to find ways to locate asteroids heading toward Earth early enough to be able to do something about them. Then they need to invent some way of preventing the eventual impact.

"Out in space, there are some pretty big mountains on the loose."

—— American scientist and author Isaac Asimov, 1979

Astronomers and other scientists worry about an asteroid smashing into Earth. They are devising ways to prevent that catastrophe.

Blowing up an approaching asteroid would be a bad idea. It would only change a single object into dozens or perhaps hundreds of objects, all of which would collide with Earth. This could be worse than a single impact. A better idea would be to change the orbit of the object so it misses Earth. A small nudge to an asteroid still some distance from Earth could cause it to miss Earth by thousands of miles by the time it reached the planet's vicinity. This could be done in many ways. A rocket could be attached to one side of the asteroid. Its thrust would change the asteroid's path. Even something as simple as setting off an explosion on one side of the asteroid could be enough.

To avoid an asteroid impact, we also need to know where the asteroids are. To deal with this, NASA has established a Near-Earth Object Program. The purpose of the program is to detect and track potentially hazardous asteroids and comets that might approach Earth. The goal is to locate at least 90 percent of the asteroids and comets that pass near Earth. So far, more than six thousand near-Earth objects have been found. More than one thousand of them are asteroids with a diameter of approximately 0.5 miles (0.8 km) in size or larger. Of these, 145 have been determined to be potentially hazardous. This does not mean that these asteroids *will* hit Earth, but it's a possibility. By closely watching these asteroids and keeping track of changes in their orbits, NASA can better predict the chances that one of them might be come a threat.

5 The Perseid
METEOR SHOWER

Streaks of light from a meteor shower fill the sky, to the wonder of watchers on Earth.

A HALF-DOZEN TIMES EACH YEAR, HUMANS ON EARTH ARE TREATED TO A SPECTACULAR NATURAL FIREWORKS SHOW. THE NIGHT SKY IS FILLED WITH DOZENS OR EVEN HUNDREDS OF DAZZLING STREAKS OF LIGHT. PEOPLE SOMETIMES CALL THESE STREAKS FALLING STARS OR SHOOTING STARS. BUT THEY ARE NOT STARS AT ALL. THEY ARE JUST TINY BITS OF ROCK AND METAL.

Like asteroids, some meteoroids are leftover material from the formation of the solar system. Other meteoroids are fragments from colliding asteroids. The debris from old comets forms meteoroids too. Comets leave behind a cloud of dust and pieces of gravel as they fall apart. Most bits are no larger than a grain of sand or a pea.

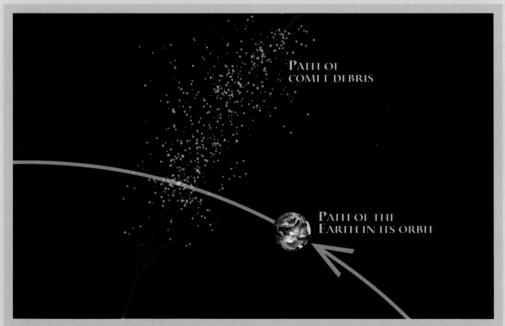

PATH OF COMET DEBRIS

PATH OF THE EARTH IN ITS ORBIT

When tiny grains of rock from a comet hit Earth's atmosphere, they heat up and begin to glow, creating a meteor shower.

The solar system is filled with little particles like these. They are too small to be of any harm to Earth-dwellers. But any body that does not have a protective atmosphere, such as the Moon, is bombarded by these particles every day. Mountains on the Moon are very smooth and rounded. This is because, over millions of years, its rugged mountains were sandblasted by the fall of tiny meteoroids.

When these tiny grains of rock and metal hit Earth's atmosphere at speeds of up to 44 miles (71 km) per second, they are almost instantly burned up by friction. This produces a brilliant flash of light that can be seen from miles away. Most of the meteors streaking through the night sky are 45 to 60 miles (72 to 97 km) above Earth's surface.

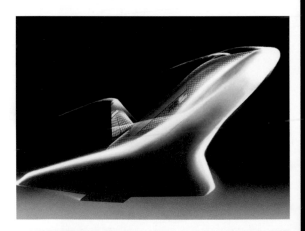

Just like the small rocks that pass Earth during meteor showers, the space shuttle glows during its reentry to Earth. The glow is caused by friction on the exterior of the space shuttle in Earth's atmosphere.

EARTH'S *Protective Shield*

Friction can create heat. Just rub the palms of your hands together. They will quickly grow warm. Rubbing two pieces of wood together can make them get hot enough to catch fire, as any Boy or Girl Scout can demonstrate. You might not think that air could create as much friction. But if you move through it fast enough, it can. Astronauts returning from space in the space shuttle hit the atmosphere at more than 17,000 miles (27,358 km) per hour. Friction heats the outside of the shuttle to a temperature of 3,000°F (1,650°C). The shuttle has to have a special surface to resist such heat. Even then it grows red hot before the friction finally slows it down. Meteoroids hit the atmosphere at speeds ranging from 24,000 miles (38,624 km) per hour to 159,000 miles (255,890 km) per hour. At such speeds, all but the very biggest meteoroids burn up long before nearing the ground. A meteoroid has to be at least as large as a marble for even a tiny portion of it to reach Earth's surface. Anything smaller will burn up in the atmosphere about 50 to 75 miles (80 to 121 km) above Earth.

MAIN METEOR SHOWERS

Shower name	Constellation Associated with It	Date of Greatest Number of Meteors	Duration in days	Average number per hour	Associated comet
Lyrid	Lyra	April 21	4	8	None
Perseid	Perseus	August 12	25	70	Comet 1862 III
Orionid	Orion	October 21	14	20	Comet Halley
Taurid	Taurus	November 7	variable	15	Comet Encke
Leonid	Leo	November 16	7	20	Comet P/Tempel-Tuttle
Geminid	Gemini	December 12	5.2	50	3200 Phaethon

Fragments from the Leonid meteor shower flash over Mount Fuji in Japan in November 1998.

A meteor from the Geminid meteor shower streaks through the New York sky in December 2009. The Geminid shower appears every December with as many as fifty meteor flashes during its show.

On an average night, you might see three meteors an hour. Several times every year, a meteor shower occurs. During these showers, as many as sixty meteors may flash by every hour. Most recurring meteor showers are caused by the debris from comets. Comets leave behind clouds of dust and gravel, like the trail of exhaust behind a speeding car. Because these clouds follow the orbit of the original comets, they return at predictable intervals, just as the comets do.

The meteor showers are named after the constellation they appear to come from. The meteors don't really come from the constellations, however. The star formations are just in the background. They are trillions of miles away, while the meteors are probably less than 100 miles (161 km) away.

"Meteors are the embers of comets."
—Fritz Kahn, German science writer and illustrator, 1954

A Superstition?

Humans have seen meteors streaking through the night sky for tens of thousands of years. And occasionally a rock might be found, one that seemed out of place among all the rest of the rocks in an area. It was not until the early nineteenth century that anyone suggested there might be a connection.

In 1794 a German scientist named Ernst F. F. Chladni suggested that meteorites did indeed fall out of the sky. Most other scientists thought this was ridiculous. But in 1803, a meteoroid exploded over a town in southern France. Hundreds of people witnessed a shower of stones falling to the ground afterward. The news was sent to the Academy of Sciences in Paris. The scientists there scoffed at it, declaring the idea that stones might fall from the sky nothing but superstitious nonsense.

A Frenchman named Jean-Baptiste Biot was a very careful, much respected scientist. When he turned in his report about the 1803 fall of stones and declared that what the people had seen was true, he was believed. Finally, the fact that stones fell from the sky was taken seriously.

In 1807 a stone was seen to fall from the sky in Connecticut. Two scientists asked the government for permission to excavate it. President Thomas Jefferson—himself an enthusiastic amateur scientist—refused to grant them the money. He didn't know of Biot's report and thought it impossible that a rock could fall out of the sky.

Top: *Ernst F. F. Chladni, a German scientist, mostly studied sound. But in 1794, he suggested that meteorites were rocks that fell from the sky.*
Bottom: *The respected French scientist Jean-Baptiste Biot confirmed that the shower of stones that fell on a French town in 1803 had come from the sky.*

A Cosmic Shooting Gallery

Cars, houses, and even people are occasionally hit by meteoroids that reach the ground. Over the past two hundred years, there have been dozens of reports. In 1954 a 9-pound (4-kilogram) meteoroid crashed through the roof of a house in Alabama. It hit the woman living there, leaving a huge bruise on her hip. In 1994, in Spain, a falling meteoroid broke the windshield and bent the steering wheel of a moving car. The driver was not hurt, only surprised. A meteorite about the size of a tennis ball hit a building in Virginia in January 2010. No one was hurt, but the building was damaged by the impact. The meteor was a fragment of a larger meteor that had been seen as far north as New Jersey.

A meteorite hit this home in Indonesia in May 2010. The family wasn't home at the time.

Meteorites from the Moon and Mars

Very, very rarely, a meteorite found on Earth is not a piece of an asteroid or a remnant of an old comet. It is a piece of the Moon or Mars. In the distant past, the planets were bombarded constantly by large asteroids. Some of these hit the Moon and Mars so hard that the explosion threw material from these bodies out into space. Eventually, some of it found its way to Earth. Scientists can tell the difference between ordinary meteorites and those that may have come from another planet. The composition of a meteorite from the Moon will resemble other lunar rocks.

THE LARGEST Meteorite

The largest known meteorite lies on the farm where it was found in the African nation of Namibia. Known as the Hoba meteorite, it is a mass of iron weighing more than 60 tons (54 metric tons). The largest meteorite on display in the United States is the Willamette meteorite at the American Museum of Natural History in New York City. It is an iron meteorite 10 feet (3.15 m) long and 5 feet (1.5 m) high, weighing 15 tons (13 metric tons).

Most rocks blown off the Moon eventually are captured by Earth's gravity. After orbiting Earth for tens of thousands of years, they finally come close enough to fall into Earth's atmosphere. If the rock is large enough, it survives to reach the ground. Because the composition of Earth and the Moon are very similar, meteorites from the Moon look a lot like Earth rocks. Scientists can tell the difference, though, because lunar meteorites show signs of having melted while passing through the atmosphere. They also contain rare radioactive

The largest known meteorite on Earth, the Hoba meteorite, weighs more than 60 tons (54 metric tons). It was found at Hoba West farm in Namibia, Africa.

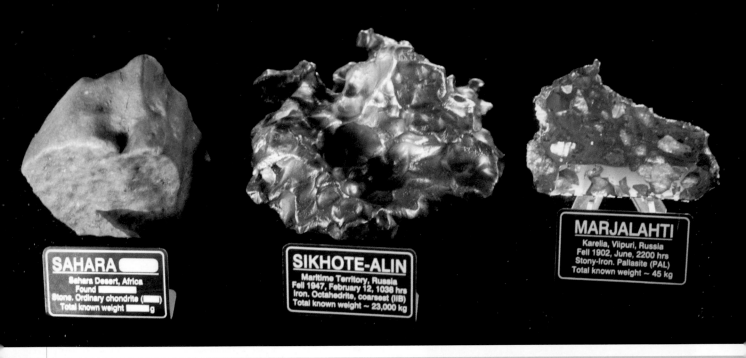

SAHARA
Sahara Desert, Africa
Found ▮▮▮▮
Stone. Ordinary chondrite (▮▮▮▮)
Total known weight ▮▮▮▮ g

SIKHOTE-ALIN
Maritime Territory, Russia
Fell 1947, February 12, 1038 hrs
Iron. Octahedrite, coarsest (IIB)
Total known weight ~ 23,000 kg

MARJALAHTI
Karelia, Viipuri, Russia
Fell 1902, June, 2200 hrs
Stony-Iron. Pallasite (PAL)
Total known weight ~ 45 kg

Meteorites come in many shapes and sizes. These are three from a private collection.

materials created only while a stone is passing through outer space. Also, the Moon contains certain elements in amounts different from the amount of those elements on Earth.

Meteorites from the Moon are very rare. Out of the tens of thousands of meteorites found, only 130 are known to have come from the Moon.

Even rarer are meteorites from Mars. Only thirty-four meteorites have been proven to be from that planet. One thirteen-thousand-year-old Martian meteorite was found to contain microscopic wormlike objects. Many scientists believe these may be fossil microbes. If this is true, then it is evidence that life may once have existed on Mars.

Meteor showers are not only beautiful to see, they are also a reminder that space is not empty. The Earth in its orbit is like a ship navigating a shallow sea full of rocks. Most of these rocks are completely harmless. The only result of running into them is a sky filled with fireworks.

"I would more easily believe that [a] Yankee [Northern] professor would lie than that stones would fall from heaven."

—U.S. President Thomas Jefferson, upon being informed that a meteorite found in 1807 had fallen from the sky, 1808

COLLECTING
Meteoroid Dust

Gather these supplies:

- Cookie sheet
- Plastic wrap
- Magnet
- Sheet of paper
- Magnifying glass

Line the cookie sheet with the plastic wrap. Fold the edges of the wrap under the sheet, so it won't blow away. Place it outdoors in a place where nothing blocks the sky and the sheet is protected from the wind. Let the sheet remain outdoors for at least a week. When you bring it back inside, the plastic will be covered with all sorts of debris. There may be leaves, grass, dead bugs, and many other things. Carefully run the magnet through all this. (A piece of paper wrapped over the end of the magnet will make it easier to remove whatever sticks to it.) Most likely, at least a few small particles will stick to the magnet. These are the remnants of meteoroids that disintegrated in the upper atmosphere. They stick to the magnet because most meteoroids have iron and nickel in them. Look at the particles through the magnifying glass. What do they look like? Compare them to the ones in the picture to the right. Meteoroid dust like this adds hundreds if not thousands of tons (metric tons) of weight to Earth every day.

Microscopic bits of meteoroids like these might be found in collected space dust. Do the experiment at left to see how it works.

THE
Kuiper Belt

This is an imagined view of the icy Kuiper Belt object called Sedna. It is more than eighty times farther from the Sun than Earth.

In 1951 American astronomer Gerard Kuiper suggested that the solar system might be surrounded by a vast region of icy bodies. The region stretches from within the orbit of Pluto, which is about thirty times farther from the Sun than Earth, to about fifty times farther from the Sun. Most of these icy bodies are very small, but a few are as large as Pluto or larger. Many scientists believe that Pluto itself may be just an unusually large Kuiper Belt body.

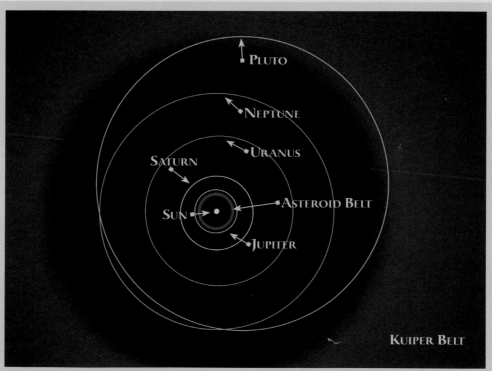

The Kuiper Belt is a vast region of orbiting icy bodies beyond the solar system.

By the end of the 1990s, more than two dozen large objects had been found in the Kuiper Belt. They range in size from 60 miles (97 km) to 472 miles (760 km) wide. These objects are called plutinos because of their resemblance to Pluto.

The Kuiper Belt is made of material left over from the formation of the solar system. When the solar system was still mostly dust and gas, heavier materials, such as rocks and metal, tended to move toward the Sun. Lighter materials, such as ice, wound up in the outer reaches. Imagine a mixture of sawdust and iron filings poured into a glass of water. The iron filings would sink to the bottom, and the sawdust would float. Something like this happened during the formation of the solar system. It's why heavier, rocky planets such as Mercury, Venus, Earth, and Mars, are found close to the Sun. Lighter planets made of gas and liquid, such as Jupiter, Saturn, Uranus, and Neptune, are found farther away.

Most of the icy bodies in the solar system can be found beyond Pluto. The Kuiper Belt is filled with them. It may hold as many as 200 million ice bodies the size of Halley's comet and as many as 6.7 billion smaller ones. Every now and then, one of these chunks of ice is disturbed from its orbit. It then begins a long, long fall toward the Sun. When this happens, the icy body becomes a comet.

The American astronomer Gerard Kuiper first suggested in 1951 that a belt of icy bodies similar to Pluto existed at the edges of the solar system.

"The outermost solar system, beyond Neptune, turns out to be full of small bodies, some approaching Pluto in size."
—William K. Hartmann, U.S. astronomer, 2005

FACTS ABOUT SOME
Kuiper Belt Objects

Name	Average Distance from Sun	Size in diameter	Length of Time to Orbit the Sun
Eris	6.3 billion miles (10.1 billion km)	1,522 miles (2,450 km)	557 years
Pluto	3.7 billion miles (6 billion km)	1,413 miles (2,274 km)	248 years
Sedna	Between 76 and 940 times the Earth's distance from the Sun	About 930 miles (1,497 km)	12,000 years
Makemake	4.5 billion miles (7.2 billion km)	800 to 1,180 miles (1,287 to 1900 km)	310 years
Quaoar	4 billion miles (6.4 billion km)	783 miles (1260 km)	285 years
Varuna	4.2 billion miles (6.75 billion km)	500 miles (805 km)	283 years

This computer-generated image compares the sizes of the three dwarf planets—(left to right) Eris, Pluto, and Ceres—to Earth (below right).

GIANT KUIPER BELT OBJECTS

In 2002 scientists discovered an object in the Kuiper Belt that they named Quaoar. It orbits a billion miles farther from the Sun than Pluto. At 783 miles (1,260 km) across, it is about half the size of Pluto. Until the discovery of Quaoar, the largest Kuiper Belt object was Varuna, at 500 miles (805 km) wide. Most Kuiper Belt objects are comet-sized—that is, only about 0.3 to 12 miles (0.5 to 19 km) wide. Quaoar is almost seventy times larger than any known comet.

Quaoar even has a tiny moon of its own called Weywot. It may be a fragment of Quaoar knocked off by the impact of an asteroid or another Kuiper Belt object.

Since then many more large Kuiper Belt objects have been discovered. Sedna is about 930 miles (1,497 km) in diameter. It was discovered in 2003.

This illustration shows the three dwarf planets of the solar system and twelve other dwarf planet candidates, plus Pluto's moon Charon—all compared to the size of Earth.

ERIS

MAKEMAKE

HAUMEA

SEDNA

QUAOAR

VARUNA

CERES

PALLAS

VESTA

HYGÉIA

MOON

EARTH

PLUTO

CHARON

EGG-SHAPED
Kuiper Belt Object

The Kuiper Belt object known as 2003 EL61 is unlike any other one. While Pluto, Eris, and Sedna are round like Earth, 2003 EL61 is shaped like an egg. It is large, about 1,217 × 944 × 621 miles (1,959 × 1519 × 999 km). Its shape is probably the result of its fast spin. It makes one turn every 3.9 hours, faster than any known body in the solar system. Also, 2003 EL61 has two moons. The larger, outer one is about 217 miles (349 km) wide and orbits every forty-nine days. The smaller, inner moon takes just thirty-nine days to swing around 2003 EL61.

So far, it is the most distant object discovered orbiting the Sun. Probably half ice and half rock, Sedna is more than three times farther away from the Sun than Pluto—more than 990 times farther away than Earth. From that distance, the Sun would be only a bright star in the sky.

One of the largest Kuiper Belt objects was found in 2005. Makemake is about three-fourths the size of Pluto. Like many other Kuiper Belt objects, its surface is covered with frozen methane, ethane, and nitrogen. Makemake is 52 times farther from the Sun than Earth. It receives 250 times less light and heat from the Sun than Earth does. This makes Makemake a dark, cold world.

> *"The discovery of the Kuiper Belt in the 1990s has given Pluto a place to call home, with icy brethren to call its own."*
>
> —Neil deGrasse Tyson, U.S. astronomer, 2009

Eris is the largest Kuiper Belt object of all. Discovered in 2003, it is about 1,522 miles (2,450 km) wide, slightly larger than Pluto. Its distance from the Sun averages about three times that of Pluto. In 2005 it was discovered that Eris has a tiny moon. Astronomers named it Dysnomia. It is about one-eighth the size of Eris.

THE SMALLEST
Kuiper Belt Object

In December 2009, Hubble Space Telescope scientists found the smallest Kuiper Belt object yet. The unnamed body is only about 3,200 feet (975 m) wide. It orbits the Sun at a distance of 4.2 billion miles (6.8 billion km). That's about forty-five times farther from the Sun than Earth. Like most other Kuiper Belt objects, this one probably is made almost entirely of ice.

This is how a artist imagined this landscape on Makemake. It is a giant Kuiper Belt object orbiting more than thirty-eight times farther from the Sun than Earth. The temperature there is a frigid –397°F (–238°C).

Exploration of the Kuiper Belt has only just begun. It may hold objects larger, smaller, and more unique than any yet discovered.

BEYOND THE KUIPER BELT

Many scientists believe that beyond the Kuiper Belt lies something called the Oort cloud. It is made up of billions of icy bodies that surround the Sun in an immense sphere. This sphere extends to about 18 trillion miles (29 trillion km)

Above: *This illustration shows the view from the outer edge of the Oort cloud, fifty thousand times farther from the Sun than Earth. The bright ring around the Sun is the Kuiper Belt.*
Left: *Jan Oort was the Dutch astronomer who in 1950 suggested that icy bodies surrounded the Sun beyond the Kuiper Belt. The Oort cloud was named for him.*
Below: *This diagram shows the Sun and solar system, with the Oort cloud surrounding them.*

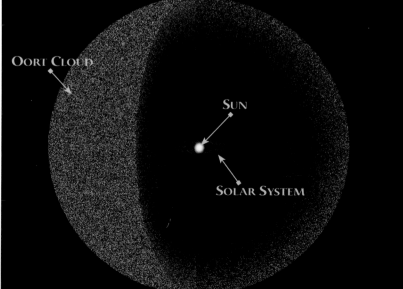

OORT CLOUD

SUN

SOLAR SYSTEM

from the Sun. This is a distance more than two hundred thousand times farther than Earth is from the Sun. From one of the icy bodies in the Oort cloud, the distant Sun would be lost among all the other stars in the sky.

Many scientists believe that the Oort cloud is another place where comets originate. Every now and then one of the icy bodies in the cloud is disturbed—perhaps by the gravity of a distant star—and begins its long journey toward the Sun.

The Oort cloud is named for the Dutch astronomer Jan Oort, who first suggested its existence in 1950. The outer edge of the Oort cloud is thought to be the farthest limit of the solar system. Beyond this region, the influence of the Sun ends and interstellar space begins.

7 Pluto AND CHARON

This digital image shows Pluto (right) and its moon, Charon, orbit on the fringes of the solar system. The distant Sun (far left) looks like a bright star.

$\mathcal{J}$UST WHERE DO PLUTO AND ITS MOON, CHARON, FIT IN? ARE THEY ASTEROIDS, COMETS, KUIPER BELT OBJECTS OR SOMETHING ELSE? FROM THE VERY MOMENT PLUTO WAS DISCOVERED IN 1930, IT HAS BEEN A MYSTERY. IT IS SO FAR AWAY AND SO SMALL THAT VERY LITTLE IS KNOWN ABOUT IT. EVEN A TELESCOPE AS POWERFUL AS THE HUBBLE SPACE TELESCOPE CAN MAKE OUT ONLY A SMALL, BLURRY BLOB WITH TANTALIZING LIGHT AND DARK AREAS.

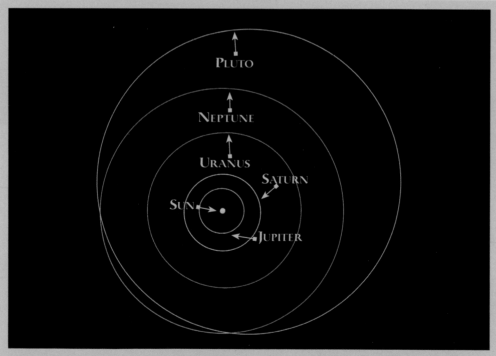

Pluto is small and has a cometlike orbit.

What is certain is that Pluto is a frigid, dark world. The Sun, seen from a distance forty times that between it and Earth, looks only like an intensely bright star. It would provide Pluto with only 1/1,500th the amount of light and heat Earth receives. A full moon provides more heat and light on Earth than the Sun does on Pluto. Pluto's dim surface is covered with frozen nitrogen ice mixed with a little frozen methane and carbon monoxide—the same gas in car exhaust. Pluto's distance from the Sun changes drastically over the course of its year, which is 90,589 days long. When its orbit carries it closest to the Sun, warmth from the Sun causes some of the ice on Pluto's surface to turn into gas. This creates a thin, temporary atmosphere of nitrogen. When Pluto is most distant from the Sun, the nitrogen freezes again and Pluto is as airless as the Moon.

This portrait of Pluto was compiled from photos taken in 2002 and 2003. The image isn't clear enough to show whether Pluto has craters and mountains, but it does show Pluto's various colors.

"It used to be said that Pluto was a misfit. Now it turns out that Earth is the misfit. Most planets in the solar system look like Pluto, and not like the terrestrial [rocky] planets."
—*Alan Stern, principal NASA investigator, New Horizons Pluto mission, 2006*

CHARON

Perhaps the most astonishing discovery made about Pluto was that it has a moon. The moon was not discovered until 1978. Charon orbits Pluto in the same time it takes for Pluto to make one rotation. This means that Charon hangs permanently in one place in Pluto's sky, never rising or setting. If there are any creatures living on Pluto (which is highly unlikely!), one who lived on the Charon-facing side would always have the moon in its sky. A creature living on the opposite side of Pluto would never know that Charon even existed.

Left: *The Hubble Space Telescope took this image of Pluto and Charon in 1994.*
Below: *This painting shows the surface of Pluto with its moon Charon looming above it.*

This Hubble photo of Pluto and Charon includes Pluto's two smaller moons, Nix and Hydra.

Charon is a very large moon, at least in comparison to Pluto. It is nearly half the size of the planet, larger in comparison to its world than any other moon in the solar system. Earth's Moon, which is the next largest in comparison to its planet, is only one-quarter the size of Earth. Charon is so large that it might be best to describe the Pluto-Charon system as a double world. Since Charon also orbits very near Pluto, it looms very large in Pluto's sky. It would appear to be eight times wider than a full moon back on Earth. From Charon, Pluto would look even larger. It would be a huge ball seventeen times larger than a full moon.

Pluto has two other moons. They are named Nix and Hydra. They are a lot smaller than Charon and orbit much farther away. They are only about 30 to 37 miles (48 to 60 km) in diameter.

IS PLUTO A PLANET?

Astronomers disagree as to whether Pluto should really be classified as a planet. Scientists have presented some good reasons why it shouldn't. Unlike all the other planets, Pluto's orbit takes it inside the orbit of Neptune.

MISSION TO *Pluto*

On January 19, 2006, NASA launched the *New Horizons* spacecraft toward Pluto. The fastest spacecraft ever launched from Earth, it will still take nine years to reach the distant little world. In addition to cameras and instruments, *New Horizons* carries some of the ashes of astronomer Clyde Tombaugh, who discovered Pluto in 1930.

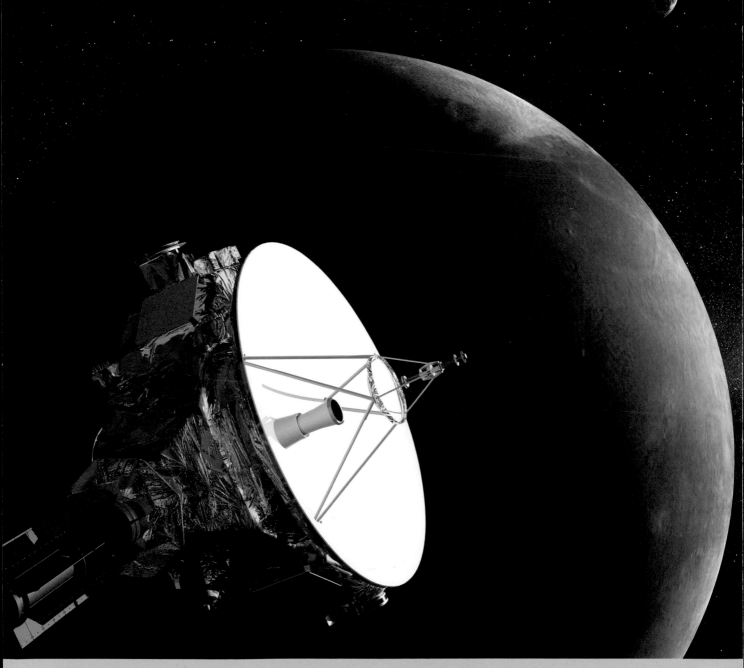

"Just as a Chihuahua is still a dog, these ice dwarfs are still planetary bodies. . . . The Pluto-like objects are more typical in our solar system than the nearby planets we first knew."

—Alan Stern, principal NASA investigator, New Horizons Pluto mission, 2006

NASA launched the New Horizons *spacecraft in 2006. This artist's rendering shows the craft approaching Pluto in 2015.*

Pluto (far right) *takes its place as a Kuiper Belt object in this painting.*

Then, for a while, Neptune is the most distant planet from the Sun. Pluto's orbit is also tipped in relation to most of the other planets.

During the course of Pluto's long year, it passes high above the other planets and then swings below them. This kind of orbit is much more like that of a comet than any of the planets.

Instead of being made of rock and metal like Mercury, Earth, Venus, and Mars, Pluto is almost two-thirds solid ice, with a rocky core. In this respect, it resembles the gas giants and many of their moons. Pluto's thick layer of ice can be considered equivalent to a gas giant's thick atmosphere, but frozen solid.

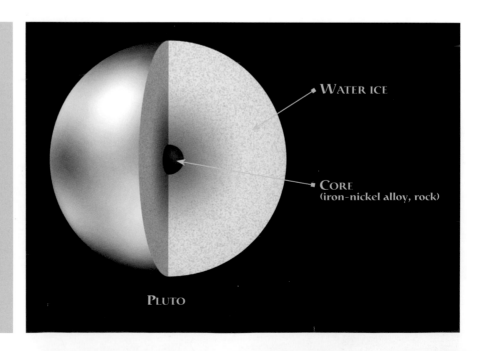

Although Pluto has a core of metal and rock, it is mainly made of ice.

WATER ICE

CORE
(iron–nickel alloy, rock)

PLUTO

FACTS ABOUT *Pluto and Charon*

PLUTO

Maximum distance from the Sun:
4.6 billion miles (7.4 billion km)

Minimum distance from the Sun:
2.8 billion miles (4.5 billion km)

Average distance from the Sun:
3.7 billion miles (5.9 billion
km), almost forty times the
distance of Earth from the Sun

Diameter: 1,413 miles (2,274 km)

CHARON

Distance from Pluto: 12,203
miles (19,638 km)

Diameter: 750 miles (1,207 km)

Pluto is also much smaller than any of the other planets and only about two-thirds the size of Earth's Moon. It is only two and a half times the size of Ceres, the largest asteroid. When Ceres was discovered in the nineteenth century, it was at first classified as a planet, but its small size caused it to be downgraded to an asteroid.

Pluto, because of its differences from other planets, recently suffered a similar fate. Many astronomers feel that Pluto is simply an unusually large member of the Kuiper Belt. These astronomers have classed Pluto—along with Eris, Sedna, Quaoar, and others—as plutoids, or dwarf planets. But other astronomers disagree. They still consider Pluto as much a planet as Earth, Mars, and Jupiter.

Meanwhile, Pluto is a kind of signpost. It marks the end of the the familiar planets in the solar system and the beginning of a frontier of mysterious, frozen worlds.

TIMELINE

240 B.C. Chinese astronomers are the first to record the appearance of Halley's comet.

A.D. 1000s Halley's comet is depicted on the Bayeux Tapestry, a record of the Norman Conquest of England in 1066.

1759 Halley's comet appears on March 13, as predicted by Edmond Halley.

1801 Giuseppe Piazzi discovers the asteroid Ceres on January 1.

1803 Jean-Baptiste Biot discovers the extraterrestrial origin of meteorites.

1950 Jan Oort develops his theory about a spherical cloud of comets surrounding the solar system.

1951 Gerard Kuiper suggests that a belt of icy bodies orbits the Sun just beyond the orbit of Neptune.

1991 On October 29, asteroid 951 Gaspra is the first asteroid to be closely approached by a spacecraft when *Galileo* makes a fly-by.

1994 More than twenty fragments of Comet Shoemaker-Levy 9 crash into Jupiter on July 16–22.

2001 The NEAR (Near Earth Asteroid Rendezvous) *Shoemaker* spacecraft lands on the asteroid 433 Eros on February 12.

2002 On June 4, astronomers discover Quaoar, a large object beyond Pluto.

2004 In January the *Stardust* spacecraft collects particles from the coma of Comet Wild 2 and returns the samples to Earth in January 2006.

2005 Astronomers discover Eris, the largest of the Kuiper Belt objects, in January.

2005 The *Deep Impact* comet probe launches an impactor at the nucleus of Comet Tempel on July 4. The explosion gives scientists much data about the composition of the comet.

2006 On January 6, the *New Horizons* spacecraft is launched toward Pluto. It will arrive in 2015.

2007 The *Dawn* spacecraft launches on September 27. Its mission is to explore the asteroid belt.

2009 A small asteroid explodes over Indonesia in October.

2009 In December astronomers discover the smallest Kuiper Belt object yet observed.

CHOOSE AN EIGHTH WONDER

Now that you've read *Seven Wonders of Asteroids, Comets, and Meteors*, do a little research to choose an eighth wonder. You may enjoy working with a friend. To start your research, look at some of the websites and books listed on the following pages. Use the Internet and library books to find more information. Think about things that

- *asteroids yet to be discovered*
- *other space objects that resemble Pluto*
- *what might lie beyond the Oort cloud*

See if you can come up with some candidates for an eighth wonder!

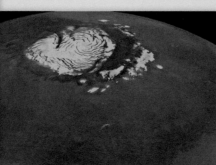

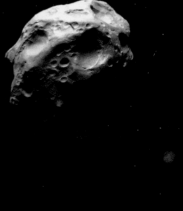

GLOSSARY AND PRONUNCIATION GUIDE

asteroid: a rocky or metallic interplanetary object, usually larger than 33 feet (10 m) in diameter

asteroid belt: a region between the orbits of Mars and Jupiter containing thousands of asteroids

coma (KOH-muh): the atmosphere of dust and gas that surrounds the nucleus of a comet

comet: an icy interplanetary body. When heated by the Sun after entering the inner solar system, it releases gases that form a bright head and long tail.

crater: a bowl-shaped depression created by the impact of a meteoroid or asteroid

Earthgrazer: see near-Earth object below

fireball: an unusually bright meteor

Kuiper (KYE-puhr) Belt: a region of space extending outward from the orbit of Pluto that contains thousands of icy bodies

meteor: the streak of light in the sky made by a meteoroid entering the atmosphere of Earth

meteorite: a meteoroid after it has landed on Earth

meteoroid: a particle in space, usually smaller than a few feet in size

meteor shower: a concentrated group of meteors, seen when Earth's orbit crosses the debris of a comet

near-Earth object (NEO): an asteroid that crosses or comes very near the orbit of the Earth. Also known as an Earthgrazer.

nucleus: the solid body at the head of a comet

Oort cloud: a sphere of icy bodies surrounding the outer solar system

Quaoar (KWAH-ohr): a Kuiper Belt object

solar system: the Sun and everything that orbits it

solar wind: the stream of gas emitted by the Sun

Source Notes

10 Carl Sagan, *Cosmos* (New York: Random House, 1980), 87.

13 Fritz Kahn, *Design of the Universe* (New York: Crown Publishers, 1954), 223.

19 Isaac Asimov, *A Choice of Catastrophes* (New York: Fawcett Columbine, 1979), 145.

20 ThinkExist, "Asteroid Quotes," *ThinkExist.com Quotations*, 2010, http://thinkexist.com/quotes/with/keyword/asteroid/ (May 5, 2010).

24 Albert Bigelow Paine, *Mark Twain: A Biography* (New York: Harper & Bros., 1912), 1,511.

24 Beatty. J. Kelly (ed), *The New Solar System* (Cambridge, MA: Sky Publishing Corp., 1999), 64.

32 Don Brownlee, "Stardust: A Mission with Many Scientific Surprises," *NASA*, October 29, 2009, http://stardust.jpl.nasa.gov/news/news116.html (December 31, 2009).

36 William K. Hartmann, *Astronomy: The Cosmic Journey* (Belmont, CA: Wadsworth, 1982), 218.

42 Asimov, *A Choice of Catastrophes*, 146.

48 Kahn, *Design of the Universe*, 238.

52 Hartmann, *Astronomy*, 218.

56 Ron Miller and William K. Hartmann, *The Grand Tour* (New York: Workman, 2005), 188.

60 ThinkExist, "Neil deGrasse Tyson Quotes," *ThinkExist.com Quotations*, 2010, http://thinkexist.com/quotation/the-discovery-of-the-kuiper-belt-in-the-s-has/1356104.html (December 9, 2009).

66 ThinkExist, "AlanSterns Quotes," *ThinkExist.com Quotations*, 2010, http://thinkexist.com/quotes/alan_stern/ (January 21, 2010).

69 Ibid.

SELECTED BIBLIOGRAPHY

Beatty, J. Kelly, Carolyn Collins Petersen, and Andrew Chaikin, eds. *The New Solar System.* Cambridge, MA: Sky Publishing Corp, 1999.

Faure, Gunter, and Teresa Mensing. *Introduction to Planetary Science.* Dortrecht, Netherlands: Springer Verlag, 2007.

Hartmann, William K. *Astronomy: The Cosmic Journey.* Belmont, CA: Wadsworth Publishing Co., 1985.

——. *Moons and Planets.* Belmont, CA: Wadsworth Publishing Co., 1999.

Miller, Ron, and William K. Hartmann, *The Grand Tour.* New York: Workman, 2005.

FURTHER READING AND WEBSITES

Books

Alvarez, Walter. T. rex *and the Crater of Doom.* Princeton, NJ: Princeton University Press, 1997. This is the story behind the discovery that the impact of a giant asteroid may have wiped out the dinosaurs.

Davies, John. *Beyond Pluto.* New York: Cambridge University Press, 2001. The book is all about the Kuiper Belt and the Oort cloud.

Koppes, Stephen N. *Killer Rocks from Outer Space.* Minneapolis: Twenty-First Century Books, 2003. The author discusses the potential danger of asteroid impacts.

Mist, Rosalind. *Could An Asteroid Hit Earth?* Chicago: Heinemann-Raintree, 2005. This book talks about the possibility of future asteroid impacts on Earth.

Moskin, Marietta D. *Sky Dragons and Flaming Swords.* New York: Walker and Co., 1985. This pictorial history of comets and meteors shows how they were depicted in art and culture.

Olson, Roberta J. M. *Fire and Ice.* Washington, DC: Smithsonian Institution, 1985. This is a good introduction to the subject of comets.

Silverstein, Alvin, Virginia Silverstein, and Laura Silverstein Nunn. *The Universe.* Minneapolis: Twenty-First Century Books, 2009. This book explores the planets of the solar system and worlds beyond.

Spangenberg, Ray, and Kit Moser. *A Look at Comets.* Danbury, CT: Children's Press, 2004. This book tells all about comets—what they are and where they come from.

———. *Meteors, Meteorites and Meteoroids.* Danbury, CT: Franklin Watts, 2002. Meteors, meteorites, and meteoroids are explained in this book.

Vogt, Gregory L. Earth's Spheres series. Minneapolis: Twenty-First Century Books, 2007. The books in this series give information about each of the Earth's spheres, from the inner core and mantle to the outer atmosphere and beyond.

Ward, D. J. *Exploring Mars.* Lerner Publications Company, 2007. This title in the Cool Science series looks at the cutting-edge technology used to explore the red planet.

Websites

Astronomy

http://www.astronomy.com
This is the official website for *Astronomy* magazine.

Deep Impact

http://solarsystem.nasa.gov/deepimpact/index.cfm
The official website of the Deep Impact comet mission is available at this NASA site.

NEAR Shoemaker

http://near.jhuapl.edu/
This is the official website of the NEAR Shoemaker mission to the asteroid Eros.

Nine Planets

www.nineplanets.org/
This website is filled with information and photos about the planets and their moons.

Sky & Telescope

http://www.skypub.com
This is the official website for *Sky & Telescope* magazine.

Spaceguard

http://www.cfa.harvard.edu/~marsden/SGF/
The U.S. branch of the asteroid-watching organization, Spaceguard, can be found here.

Stardust

http://stardust.jpl.nasa.gov/home/index.html
This is the official website of NASA's Stardust comet-sampling mission.

INDEX

ABOUT THE AUTHOR

Hugo Award–winning author and illustrator Ron Miller specializes in books about science. Among his various titles, he has written the Space Innovations series, *The Elements: What You Really Want to Know*, *Special Effects: An Introduction to Movie Magic*, and *Digital Art: Painting with Pixels*. His favorite subjects are space and astronomy. A postage stamp he created is currently on board a spaceship headed for Pluto. His original paintings can be found in collections all over the world. Miller lives in Virginia.

PHOTO ACKNOWLEDGMENTS

The images in this book are used with the permission of: © Ron Miller, pp. 5, 7, 12, 17, 18, 23, 24, 25 (top), 30, 32, 33 (right), 34, 35, 36 (bottom), 39 (left), 43, 44, 45, 53, 54, 55, 58, 60-61, 62 (top and bottom right), 64, 65, 67 (bottom); © Chris Butler/Photo Researchers, Inc., p. 6; © Dennis Milon/Photo Researchers, Inc., p. 8; © Mark Garlick/Photo Researchers, Inc., pp. 9, 57; William K. Hartmann Courtesy of UCLA/Newscom, p. 10; NASA images courtesy of Black Cat Studios, pp. 11 (both), 16, 27 (top), 28 (all), 29 (bottom), 31 (left), 66, 73 (top left and bottom right); NASA/ISAS/JAXA, p. 13; © CORBIS, p. 14; © John R. Foster/Photo Researchers, Inc., p. 21; © TONY MOOW/anama images/CORBIS, p. 22; © Stocktrek Images/Getty Images, pp. 25 (bottom), 29 (top), 39 (right), 69; © Hulton Archive/Getty Images, p. 26; ESO, p. 27 (center); NASA/JPL, pp. 27 (bottom), 41 (top), 59, 70 (bottom), 73 (center bottom); NASA/JPL-Caltech, p. 31 (right); © Time Life Pictures/Getty Images, p. 36 (top); NASA, p. 37; © Russell Croman/Photo Researchers, Inc., p. 38; © Dennis Milon/Visuals Unlimited, Inc., p. 41 (bottom); © SPL/Photo Researchers, Inc., pp. 46, 49 (top), 62 (bottom left); © AFP/Getty Images, p. 47; © Stan Honda/AFP/Getty Images, p. 48; © Stefano Bianchetti/CORBIS, p. 49 (bottom); © ROMEO GACAD/ AFP/Getty Images, p. 50; © Sinclair Stammers/Photo Researchers, Inc., p. 51; Ana Venegas/KRT/Newscom, p. 52; © Jack Fields/Photo Researchers, Inc., p. 56; NASA/NSSDC, p. 67 (top); © NASA/Getty Images, p. 68; © Gary Hinks/Photo Researchers, Inc., pp. 70-71; © Richard Wainscoat/Alamy, p. 73 (top center); NASA, ESA and G. Bacon (STScI), p. 73 (top right); © Startrek RF/Getty Images, p. 73 (center right); © ALI JAREKJI/ Reuters/Corbis, p. 73 (bottom left).

Front cover: NASA images courtesy of Black Cat Studios (top left); © Richard Wainscoat/Alamy (top center); NASA/JPL/University of Arizona (top right); NASA, ESA and G. Bacon (STScI) (center); © Startrek RF/Getty Images (bottom left); NASA/JPL (bottom center); © ALI JAREKJI/Reuters/Corbis (bottom right).